I Like Sign Language

Written by Carrie Pond
Photographs by John Paul Endress

Celebration Press
Parsippany, New Jersey

Hello.

Watch me!

I use sign language.
Do you want to try?
Watch me!

People

you

I / me

he / him

she / her

I like him.

Family

mother

father

sister

brother

I like my sister.

Animals

cat

dog

rabbit

frog

I like my cat.

9

Weather

hot

cold

sun

rain

I like rain.

Transportation

car

train

boat

airplane

I like boats.

Sports

baseball

basketball

soccer

swimming

I like baseball.

Good-bye!